Emotionally Unavailable Men

How to Recognize and Avoid Emotionally Unavailable Men

by Luna Parker

Table of Contents

Visit www.attractandcaptivate.com/bonus to claim this free
exclusive bonus content now.

Introduction

Emotionally unavailable men (EUMs) are some of the worst men to be in a relationship with. They don't want to form a stable bond with you; instead they choose to spend as little time as possible with you, using you for fun but not for a true connection.

If you've been in a relationship with an EUM, or have been around a few for any length of time, you'll know that they come in as many varieties as there are layers in an onion. They can't be differentiated based on looks, intelligence, tastes, age, or any other easily identifiable attributes at first glance. However they do the most damage in a relationship, and are often quite mentally and emotionally scarring to be involved with.

How, then, should you go about identifying them?

There are plenty of traits that they **do** share in common, and you will be able to identify these but only if you know where to look. And that is exactly what we'll be discussing in this book.

Just to be clear, emotional unavailability isn't particularly exclusive to men, and is found in some women as well. But since the characteristics don't change across sexes, the following red flags apply to members of both genders. Keep in mind, being an EUM also doesn't make someone a good or bad person. It's an emotional trait, one of many that constitute a person's psychological make-up. However, it doesn't change the fact that you deserve a better partner for a mature romantic relationship.

So, are you ready for this crash course that could significantly improve your dating life, and your chances of being in a healthy, happy relationship?

Let's get started!

Red Flag #1: Excessive Mystique

So, you've recently met someone who has an air of mystery about him. While the mystique may be sexy at first, everything seems to be shaded in layers of gray, and you know nothing concrete or worthwhile about him.

If you only met a few days ago, it's somewhat normal, since it takes a little time for most people to open up beyond a certain point. But, if you still feel the same way a few weeks or months after getting to know him, you're either the worst communicator on the planet (highly unlikely), or you'd better watch out. It's a massive red flag, and you're probably involved with an EUM.

EUMs love to keep their cards close to their chest. They don't open up about their work or personal lives, their history or their friends. In fact, most of what you know about them may only come from the tidbits that slip through the cracks, or from what you've gleaned through your own observations.

Since they have no desire to get emotionally close to you, they will listen to what you have to say and keep filing it away for use at a later time, when they need to draw on their knowledge of you to either manipulate you or find sweet ways out of sticky situations. But they will avoid opening up to you in any significant or meaningful way.

Getting to a point where you can meet his friends or family will feel harder than wading through quicksand and probably just about as pleasant too, since you barely know them or anything about them. In all likelihood, they'll know just as little about you too.

But, don't confuse talks of exes or past relationships with being forthcoming. Many women, when in relations with EUMs, think along the lines of, 'Oh, he's talking to me about past hurts and bonds. He must be trying to get emotionally close. He wants me to understand him better.' Please don't delude yourselves this way. Intelligent EUMs understand their lack of emotional interest quite well, and use that knowledge wisely. They don't have to marry you to enjoy your company, at least for now. So they'll drop whatever little bits of information from their past, now irrelevant since they're no longer the same person that they were, to make sure you stay on the hook.

The difference is: However well you may get to know their past, you will never know what they truly think or feel in the present.

That alone makes it absurdly easy for them to pick up and move on once they're bored of you, or meet someone else. Their present thoughts and feelings symbolize their growth in the time that you know them. They may listen to everything you have to say, because there are plenty of EUMs who take pride in being good company or good listeners, and not behaving like pigs, but they will never share their growth with you. That's because, in doing so, they would have to form an emotional bond with you, and that would make leaving at the drop of a hat much more complicated.

Let me bring up the first important piece of learning that I want to impart to you in this book: That will not change. Ever. At least, not for you. Most people have the self-delusion when they meet an EUM that if they spend enough time with or around them, they'll be able to diagnose the disease and cure their pain, thus leaving the EUM healthy enough to feel again. The EUM can feel plenty, just not for you. What they have isn't a disease, not one that you can do anything about anyway. In fact, the longer you hang around an EUM [who knows that he's an EUM], the less likely you are ever to be viewed as a serious partner.

It's much better to cut your losses at this point and leave. If the EUM is to have a change of heart at any probable point, it will be after you leave. If they come back after you, maybe there is some hope. But I would still recommend giving him a wide berth and searching for someone you don't have to play games with just to make him realize what you mean to him.

Red Flag #2: O Lover, Where Art Thou?

The cool, good-looking, well-spoken guy that you've recently met is amazing company. He knows when to listen, when to pay attention, to court or compliment you. He's always trying to make you laugh, and makes sure that you have a good time. As I mentioned, there are a lot of EUMs who understand their lack of emotional interest yet take pride in being good company. Men who misbehave with women, openly insult them or rub their lack of interest in other's faces may have the EUM trait, but more importantly are sleazebags through and through.

However, you may find that the moment your dream date leaves, he's harder to pin down than a buttered eel. He's never really around when you call him, or always manages to make a reasonable excuse, and follows up with an incredible apology later. That's a red flag.

An EUM hates being answerable to you, and so will create innumerable layers between you and him so that you never really know how to get in touch with him directly. He'll have all of the trappings of modern life - AIM, Gtalk, Twitter, Facebook, etc. for people to keep trying to get in touch with him, but when it counts, and if he's out of your sight, he probably won't respond on any of them until it's convenient for him to talk to you, and not the other way round.

When he disappears, and it may stretch for days or weeks, he will never give you reasonable explanations for what he was doing, or whether he took your emotions into account during his disappearing act. He will probably come up with a fabulous way of making up, if he does, and then shrug it off the moment he thinks you've been reasonably placated.

For an EUM, you're a chase. And a sporadic one at that, interspersed as his visits to you are when he's not involved in his real life - of which you are definitely not a part.

If you feel like the person you're involved with appears and disappears out of your life quite randomly, with messages of extreme interest on his part getting confused with complete communication black-outs, who is then flaky about any descriptive details as to his actions throughout this time, you're definitely with an EUM.

Assert your boundaries then and there, if you feel like letting this charade continue. Do not let him waltz in and out of your life so easily, and place conditions over his disappearing acts. If he's an EUM, he will most probably baulk at that idea, and may simplify things for you by showing his true colors.

However, intelligent EUMs are good at snaking their way in and out of your emotions. If you do let this charade continue, expect to get hurt. There really are no two ways about it.

Red Flag #3: Junkie Junction

EUMs may be chronic or temporary. Their state could be a result of anything from past hurts to trust issues, or they may simply have no sense of emotional attraction to you. However, if your new beau shows any signs of junkie behavior, chances are he's an EUM.

Now let me clarify this further. I'm not just talking about drugs. If your man is a compulsive drug-user, an alcoholic, an excessive gamer (differentiate between passion for a hobby and running away here; if he games a lot, but opens up to you, he's not an EUM), overtly workaholic (again, passion vs excuse to run away), or any of the other relevant 'holics', chances are he's using those mediums to bar his emotions and hide them away behind a neat little barrier, instead of dealing with them in an adult, healthy way by communicating, either with you or someone else.

Junkies mostly exist in two major frames of mind - either enjoying the high of their fix (whether it's drugs or recent professional successes), or searching for their next hit soon thereafter. They have no place in their emotional palette for you, and definitely not enough to get emotionally attached to you in any significant way. Your presence in their lives is a matter of convenience and, as soon as you stop being convenient or they find a shiny, new toy to play with, they'll move on.

So, don't become a junkie's crutch. Leave them be, and move on. Trust me, they'll have no trouble coping with it, and is that really the kind of person you want to be with?

Red Flag #4: The King of Non-Committal

The guy you've recently met is passionate, impulsive, exciting, thrilling - all those adjectives that most women love to find in a man they're with. He loves to live in the moment, and you adore every second you spend in his company because he makes you feel so alive and vibrant.

The problem is that he lives so excessively in the moment that planning a date with him a week in advance is impossible. He doesn't even stick to tomorrow's plans without a hundred different problems butting in. He has no idea about his tastes, doesn't know which foods or brands he likes the most, has no significant favorites in most things he does, because they change so suddenly and so often. Keep an eye out for this red flag. You're most likely with an EUM.

This sort of EUM is ruled by fickleness. He's like a child trapped in his favorite toy store, and most likely has no idea of who he really is and what he really wants. He's so twisted up inside with acting on his next impulse, that he can't even process his own emotions entirely, much less what his emotions are regarding you. The most frequent answers to any emotional question that you would ask him would probably be 'I don't know'.

These are also the most likely EUMs to propose the arrangement of 'Friends With Benefits' between the two of you. This allows them to enjoy your company, without any of the emotional responsibilities that it entails. After all, in most cases 'FWB' equates to 'Be my booty call'. It's an easy way of slipping in and out of your life, without needing any significant retrospect on their part as to their feelings for you, and without any need for comprehensive and satisfactory answers when they want to end things and move on.

While life may be a hoot with this EUM, it will turn sour pretty fast. EUMs are often full of silver-tongued whispers of beautiful promises, which they hardly ever follow up on. He's going to be about as reliable as a monkey guarding a banana store. The moment his impulsiveness leads his quest away from you, he will drop you like a hot potato, still shiny-eyed in his need to indulge in his next new urge.

Red Flag #5: Mr. Womanizer

The surest way to figure out a guy's an EUM is if he's constantly engaging with multiple partners. Someone who's dating a single person is usually trying to establish a deeper bond or connection with his partner, which is practically impossible to occur in multiple dating scenarios. They become more akin to games, where the player is simply chasing the high score in every life he enters.

A man who is constantly on the lookout for newer partners to hook up with while with you is in no way emotionally attached, at least not to you. Also, as I mentioned before, the longer you hang around such EUMs, the less likely you are ever to be seen as a serious partner. If you're content with your partner only sharing a part of himself with you, as he does with so many others, and without any complaint from you, why should he ever strive or want to give you any more of himself?

The answer here doesn't lie in drawing your boundaries after the fact, because if he's engaged with other people while he's been seeing you, he's already told you that you aren't important enough for him to devote himself to you. Move on. In fact, the sooner the better.

Red Flag #6: Pinging, Not Clinging

It's true that not every man enjoys cuddles after being intimate with his partner. However, even the manliest of men would want to shower you with some affection, or attention, after a particularly satisfying round of sex. It's not even a question of vulnerability, but a question of finding a way for them to put their emotions across without being 'girly' and 'mushy' about it.

However, if the man you're involved with reaches for the remote or his phone the second the two of you are done, he's about as attached to you as snails are to salt. An EUM, since he has no emotional bond with you, will have no emotions to put across after the two of you have indulged in intimacy, much less will he take your emotions or need for tender attention into consideration.

Such EUMs are not being blind to your needs; your needs simply don't figure high enough on their list of priorities to be worth devoting a few minutes to. They're inconsiderate simply because their own lack of emotional availability numbs them to any emotional needs on your part.

These EUMs are particularly scarring to get involved with. They'll make you doubt your place, damaging your self-esteem, for no good reason. Give them a wide berth, kick them out, restore your wounded pride, and move on.

Red Flag #7: Intense Self-Obsession

As I've mentioned before, EUMs will only contact you when it's convenient for them. However, for some of them, their self-obsession doesn't quite end there. Most choices between you and such an EUM will be skewed heavily in their favor - whether it's tastes, movies, food, places to meet, times to meet up, or anything else. Since their lives are mostly about their own entertainment and pleasure, with you as a tool to facilitate it all, your preferences will never be important enough to consider.

For all your efforts, they'll always act like Narcissus and you'll always be Echo - nothing but a mere mimic to their thoughts, actions and needs, without any real affection, consideration or gratitude.

Let's take this a step further as well. When you try to have a serious discussion with them, on your terms, it will always be the wrong time, wrong circumstance, wrong place, etc. The only way you'll get through that conversation without getting blasted for bringing it up is when they believe they're ready to have it and so bring it up themselves.

In fact whenever you get emotional, hurt or upset, they're likely to shut down or withdraw from you. They will also blame you for getting overtly needy or sensitive, even if you're hurt reasonably by their deeds or behavior. They will show no interest in trying to find ways to soothe you, but instead will add to your hurt before retiring to their own comfort zone so as to distance themselves from you.

If the person you're with is always following their own pace, never ready to match yours, it's a red flag. You're with an EUM.

Such EUMs will not only ignore you when it suits them, they'll also blame you for every mistake they make ('Well, it was your own fault that I cheated on you'). You'll feel like the scapegoat and the boogieman in their life, all rolled into one. It's all a load of bull though, and you'd be better off without them.

Grow a spine, kick them out of your life, and move on. You deserve better.

Red Flag #8: Past, Oh Glorious Past!

If your new beau is always talking about his past life or relationships on his own, without any relevant conversation starters or question from you (and by always, I mean always), that's a red flag if there ever was one. You're with an EUM.

Your partner is either still hooked on someone from a past relationship, or stuck in a past life. Either way, the time and moments spent with you mean very little to someone who's stuck in a loop of the past. When they're the ones always bringing it up and talking about their past constantly, their thoughts and emotions are all mired in the past as well. Whether or not they're emotionally unavailable all the time, for now, and with you, they are EUMs. And that is all that really matters.

Such people may react emotionally to you from time to time, if pushed enough, however their overall emotional make-up doesn't include you in any significant way. They need time, space, or therapy to deal with their problems. And, as much as you might wish to, there's nothing you can do to solve their issues.

You have to disengage from their baiting games and move on to find someone who has place for you in their thoughts and lives.

Red Flag #9: Catch Me If You Can

Chronic EUMs and recreational fishermen have a major trait in common - they both like to bait, catch and release. For an EUM, in the absence of an emotional bond, all that's left behind are games. EUMs delight in the thrill of a chase. They treasure each ploy and play they put in place to get someone hooked on them, physically, mentally and emotionally. However, the moment you give in and they feel like they've 'got' you, they lose interest and move onto the next chase.

If your interactions with the man you're with seem to be taking you along a never-ending emotional rollercoaster, intense highs followed by crippling lows, that's a red flag. You're almost certainly with an EUM.

While a lot of relationships have highs and lows when two people are getting to know each other better, they usually plateau after a point, barring any major upheavals. The major point to feel out here is whether it feels intentional, or like your partner relishes the highs and lows. Someone who's emotionally attached to you will be empathetic with you, and so will share your highs and lows. An EUM, on the other hand, will not.

This constant push-and-pull is likely to leave you frustrated, full of doubts, and possibly needing more attention from the man. That is the point. If you recognize any of these symptoms, you're with an EUM, and you need to detach before they bait and hook you.

Another point to mention here is that, with chronic EUMs, there's no such thing as weathering it out. You could endure for a long while, putting yourself through all the emotional turmoil that that entails, but it will most likely never change their motives. Whether it takes a month or a year, once they feel like you belong to them, they'll lose all facade of interest and move on. Don't put yourself through that unnecessary pain and anguish, stop playing their games, completely cut them out of your life, with no way back in, and move on.

Remember that, in this case, you might also make yourself more appealing to them, and they might pursue you harder. But that's precisely the reason why you need to stay away from them altogether. Chronic EUMs are more akin to predators and, even if they manage to worm their way back into your lives, their motives stay the same - bait, hook and release.

Red Flag #10: Oh Honey, It's All Yours!

If you're involved with someone who either refuses to buy things together with you, or insists that whatever the two of you purchase together be in your name, or perhaps even that everything the two of you own be neatly divided into 'yours' and 'his', ding ding ding. That's an enormous red flag. You're definitely with an EUM.

Most EUMs try to conduct things in a way that would leave no unnecessary complications and entanglements when the time comes for them to leave. Dividing all your stuff into yours and his leaves him with a neat list of things to pack up when he needs to dump you and move on. If everything is in your name, that makes this situation all the easier.

Whether or not they realize that they're doing this, EUMs hate these sorts of complications. They like to live with one foot out of the door throughout the time that you're involved with them. It's one of the easiest, and most obvious, ways to tell when someone you're close to is not really 'sharing' their space with you as you are, and is more concerned with drawing neat little boundaries through it all. And that's the trademark sign of an EUM.

Conclusion

A few basic things to remember are:

1. When someone likes you, regardless of how awkward or socially inept they might be, they'll find a way to let you know. If you're constantly insecure about the two of you, doubting everything you do, you're probably being toyed with by an EUM.

2. No matter how long a time you spend with them, if they've been EUMs while they've known you, they'll always be EUMs as far as you are concerned.

3. Putting your pride and self-esteem aside to take the emotional abuse you're subjected to by an EUM will ensure that you'll never be serious-partner material for them. If you treated someone like dirt just to toy with them, and both of you knew that's what was happening, would you truly ever respect them enough to be devoted, equal partners?

4. EUMs hate being answerable to, or responsible for,

anyone else. They will get upset when you want the simplest of answers from them, and most of what they promise will be full of hot air.

5. EUMs may show little to no interest in getting to know your friends or family. Since they have no intention of sticking around for too long, they feel no urge to entrench themselves in your lives. This may however differ from EUM to EUM.

6. There are cases when an EUM tells you that he's not emotionally ready to be involved with someone. At such points, do not attribute it to self-deprecation or playing hard-to-get. Listen intently, ask serious follow-up questions if you need to, and then move on!

7. Men may become EUMs in any number of ways. However, they always leave pain and hurt in their wake, and seldom take responsibility for their part in the troubles that they've caused, either to themselves or others. They prefer to blame their wrong-doings on others.

8. There's nothing you can do about it. Stop torturing yourself and find someone who is worthy of your time and affection. The problems and issues of an EUM aren't yours to shoulder. And, by their very nature, the more you'll stick around to try, the less they'll think of you.

Last, I'd like to thank you for purchasing this book! If you enjoyed it or found it helpful, I'd greatly appreciate it if you'd take a moment to leave a review on Amazon. Thank you!

Also, don't forget to visit the website www.attractandcaptivate.com/bonus to download this exclusive free bonus content now!

Made in United States
North Haven, CT
16 March 2022